STRESS RELIEVING PATTERNS
UNICORNS
COLORING BOOK FOR ADULT

SMILE SLOTH

Copyright 2017
Printed in The U.S.A.

TEST YOUR COLOR

1.

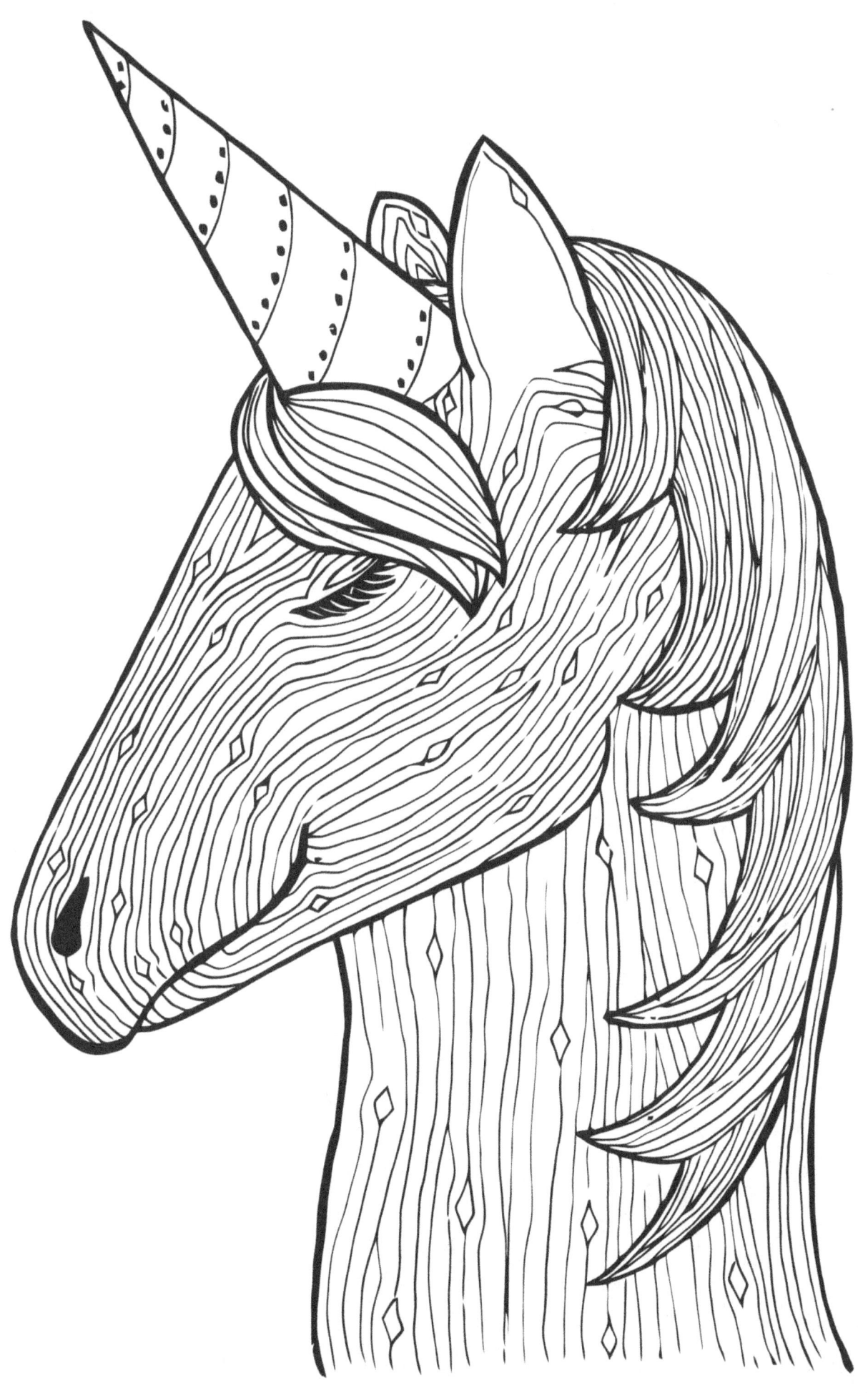

SUMMER TIME

GOOD NIGHT,
LITTLE
PRINCESS!

www.ingramcontent.com/pod-product-compliance
Lightning Source LLC
Chambersburg PA
CBHW081415280526
45788CB00009B/3119